REFLECTIONS
FOR
ADVENT

26 November – 24 December 2018

GRAHAM JAMES
GORDON MURSELL
ANGELA TILBY

with an introduction to Advent
by MARGARET WHIPP

Church House Publishing
Church House
Great Smith Street
London SW1P 3AZ

ISBN 978 1 78140 089 0

Published 2018 by Church House Publishing
Copyright © The Archbishops' Council 2018

The opinions expressed in this book are those of the
authors and do not necessarily reflect the official policy
of the General Synod or The Archbishops' Council of the
Church of England.

Liturgical editor: Peter Moger
Series editor: Hugh Hillyard-Parker
Designed and typeset by Hugh Hillyard-Parker
Copy edited by: Ros Connelly
Printed by CPI Bookmarque, Croydon, Surrey

What do you think of *Reflections for Daily Prayer*?

We'd love to hear from you – simply email us at

publishing@churchofengland.org

or write to us at

Church House Publishing, Church House,
Great Smith Street, London SW1P 3AZ.

Visit **www.dailyprayer.org.uk** for more
information on the *Reflections* series, ordering
and subscriptions.

Contents

About *Reflections for Advent*

Based on the *Common Worship Lectionary* readings for Morning Prayer, these daily reflections are designed to refresh and inspire times of personal prayer. The aim is to provide rich, contemporary and engaging insights into Scripture.

Each page lists the Lectionary readings for the day, with the main psalms for that day highlighted in **bold**. The Collect of the day – either the *Common Worship* collect or the shorter additional Collect – is also included.

For those using this book in conjunction with a service of Morning Prayer, the following conventions apply: a psalm printed in parentheses is omitted if it has been used as the opening canticle at that office; a psalm marked with an asterisk may be shortened if desired.

A short reflection is provided on either the Old or New Testament reading. Popular writers, experienced ministers, biblical scholars and theologians have contributed to this series, bringing their own emphases, enthusiasms and approaches to biblical interpretation to bear.

Regular users of Morning Prayer and *Time to Pray* (from *Common Worship: Daily Prayer*) and anyone who follows the Lectionary for their regular Bible reading will benefit from the rich variety of traditions represented in these stimulating and accessible pieces.

This volume also includes both a simple form of *Common Worship:* Morning Prayer (see pp. 35–6) and a short form of Night Prayer – also known as Compline – (see pp. 39–42), particularly for the benefit of those readers who are new to the habit of the Daily Office or for any reader while travelling.

About the authors

Stephen Cottrell is the Bishop of Chelmsford. Before this he was Bishop of Reading and has worked in parishes in London, Chichester, and Huddersfield and as Pastor of Peterborough Cathedral. He is a well-known writer and speaker on evangelism, spirituality and catechesis. His best-selling *How to Pray* (CHP) and *How to Live* (CHP) have recently been reissued.

Graham James has been Bishop of Norwich since 1999. Previously, he was Bishop of St Germans in his native Cornwall and Chaplain to the Archbishop of Canterbury. He has served on the House of Lords Select Committee on Communications, and remains the Church of England's lead spokesperson on media issues. He has been a regular contributor to BBC Radio 4's 'Thought for the Day'.

Gordon Mursell was Bishop of Stafford until his retirement in 2010. He now lives in south-west Scotland and is a writer on Christian spirituality and keen hillwalker.

Angela Tilby is a Canon Emeritus of Christ Church Cathedral, Oxford. Prior to that she served in the Diocese of Oxford following a period in Cambridge, where she was at Westcott House and St Bene't's Church. Before ordination she was a producer for the BBC, and she still broadcasts regularly.

Rachel Treweek is the Bishop of Gloucester and the first female diocesan bishop in England. She served in two parishes in London and was Archdeacon of Northolt and later Hackney. Prior to ordination she was a speech and language therapist and is a trained practitioner in conflict transformation.

Margaret Whipp is the Lead Chaplain for the Oxford University Hospitals. Her first profession was in medicine. Since ordination she has served in parish ministry, university chaplaincy, and most recently as Senior Tutor at Ripon College Cuddesdon. She writes and researches in pastoral theology, enjoys singing and long-distance pilgrimage trails, and is an Honorary Canon of Christ Church Cathedral, Oxford.

Counting the days
– A reflection on the season of Advent

An old friend recently posted a photograph of her newborn baby. He was utterly delightful, a real sweetheart, dressed in a cosy blue bodysuit with the caption across his chest: 'I've just done nine months inside.'

A baby's time from conception to birth averages 40 weeks. In that time, there is a huge amount of anatomical and physiological change, emotional and social adjustment. The slow, gradual ripening of a pregnancy proceeds at a pace that cannot be hurried. Our human gestation period of nine months is as nothing, though, compared to the time taken by other large mammals: horses take eleven months, rhinos 14 months, sperm whales 16 months, elephants famously take 22 months, while – top of the league – frilled sharks carry their young for up to three and a half years.

While each expectant mother counts the days, the seed within her womb is growing and developing its own distinctive vitality. There is a necessary sequence to its embryonic development, laid down through long ages of genetic and evolutionary wisdom. The patience of growing things rests in following this steady course of developmental progress, through which there can be no skipping of the intermediate stages. As she counts each passing day, the mother trusts and prays that her precious seed of new life, hidden deep within the womb, will slowly unfold to be a healthy and happy child. Gestation is so much a matter of patience and time.

'Above all, trust in the slow work of God,' counselled the Jesuit priest Teilhard de Chardin in one of his wartime letters. He was writing from the muddy quagmire of the trenches to a young cousin, Marguerite, who was struggling to find her way forward in life. Teilhard's advice is as relevant to expectant parents as it is to pastors and politicians, researchers and creative artists, or to young people in search of their vocation. 'We are, quite naturally, impatient in everything to reach the end without delay.' It is hard to live in the liminal space, to be in formation, en route to something unknown, something new. 'And yet it is the law of all progress that it is made by passing through some stages of instability – and that may take a very long time'.

Some of the most important things in life take a long time to ripen to maturity. Giving the necessary time to nourish our own souls, to nurture the mental and spiritual resources of others, to incubate the germ of an idea, these are the motherly tasks of many a season of pregnant waiting. Things must unfold and develop, slowly quickening and coming to birth, in their own good time. Our task, like that of a farmer, is to feed and water, and patiently tend, whatever seeds of hope God has planted for an unknown, and unimaginable future.

The season of Advent, with all its 'earnest looking forward', invites us to count the days in a spirit of watchful waiting. Against the restless busyness of the world around, Christians have good reason to slow down, to embrace a holy patience, to cherish with quiet expectancy the sweetest grace that God is bringing to birth.

Margaret Whipp

Adapted from *The Grace of Waiting*,
Norwich: Canterbury Press, 2017.

Building daily prayer into daily life

In our morning routines there are many tasks we do without giving much thought to them, and others that we do with careful attention. Daily prayer and Bible reading is a strange mixture of these. These are disciplines (and gifts) that we as Christians should have in our daily pattern, but they are not tasks to be ticked off. Rather they are a key component of our developing relationship with God. In them is *life* – for the fruits of this time are to be lived out by us – and to be most fruitful, the task requires both purpose and letting go.

In saying a daily office of prayer, we make the deliberate decision to say 'yes' to spending time with God – the God who is always with us. In prayer and attentive reading of the Scriptures, there is both a conscious entering into God's presence and a 'letting go' of all we strive to control: both are our acknowledgement that it is God who is God.

> *… come before his presence with a song…*
>
> *Know that the Lord is God;*
> *it is he that has made us and we are his;*
> *we are his people and the sheep of his pasture.*
>
> *Enter his gates with thanksgiving…*
>
> *(Psalm 100, a traditional Canticle at Morning Prayer)*

If we want a relationship with someone to deepen and grow, we need to spend time with that person. It can be no surprise that the same is true between us and God.

In our daily routines, I suspect that most of us intentionally look in the mirror; occasionally we might see beyond the surface of our external reflection and catch a glimpse of who we truly are. For me, a regular pattern of daily prayer and Bible reading is like a hard look in a clean mirror: it gives a clear reflection of myself, my life and the world in which I live. But it is more than that, for in it I can also see the reflection of God who is most clearly revealed in Jesus Christ and present with us now in the Holy Spirit.

This commitment to daily prayer is about our relationship with the God who is love. St Paul, in his great passage about love, speaks of now seeing 'in a mirror, dimly' but one day seeing face to face: 'Now I know only in part; then I will know fully, even as I have been fully known' (1 Corinthians 13.12). Our daily prayer is part of that seeing in a mirror dimly, and it is also part of our deep yearning for an ever-clearer vision of our God. As we read Scripture, the past and the future converge in the present moment. We hear words from long ago – some of which can appear strange and confusing – and yet, the Holy Spirit is living and active in the present. In this place of relationship and revelation, we open ourselves to the possibility of being changed, of being reshaped in a way that is good for us and all creation.

It is important that the words of prayer and scripture should penetrate deep within rather than be a mere veneer. A quiet location is therefore a helpful starting point. For some, domestic circumstances or daily schedule make that difficult, but it is never impossible to become more fully present to God. The depths of our being can still be accessed no matter the world's clamour and activity. An awareness of this is all part of our journey from a false sense of control to a place of letting go, to a place where there is an opportunity for transformation.

Sometimes in our attention to Scripture there will be connection with places of joy or pain; we might be encouraged or provoked or both. As we look and see and encounter God more deeply, there will be thanksgiving and repentance; the cries of our heart will surface as we acknowledge our needs and desires for ourselves and the world. The liturgy of Morning Prayer gives this voice and space.

I find it helpful to begin Morning Prayer by lighting a candle. This marks my sense of purpose and my acknowledgement of Christ's presence with me. It is also a silent prayer for illumination as I prepare to be attentive to what I see in the mirror, both of myself and of God. Amid the revelation of Scripture and the cries of my heart, the constancy of the tiny flame bears witness to the hope and light of Christ in all that is and will be.

When the candle is extinguished, I try to be still as I watch the smoke disappear. For me, it is symbolic of my prayers merging with the day. I know that my prayer and the reading of Scripture are not the smoke and mirrors of delusion. Rather, they are about encounter and discovery as I seek to venture into the day to love and serve the Lord as a disciple of Jesus Christ.

+Rachel Treweek

Lectio Divina – a way of reading the Bible

Lectio Divina is a contemplative way of reading the Bible. It dates back to the early centuries of the Christian Church and was established as a monastic practice by Benedict in the sixth century. It is a way of praying the Scriptures that leads us deeper into God's word. We slow down. We read a short passage more than once. We chew it over slowly and carefully. We savour it. Scripture begins to speak to us in a new way. It speaks to us personally, and aids that union we have with God through Christ, who is himself the Living Word.

Make sure you are sitting comfortably. Breathe slowly and deeply. Ask God to speak to you through the passage that you are about to read.

This way of praying starts with our silence. We often make the mistake of thinking prayer is about what we say to God. It is actually the other way round. God wants to speak to us. He will do this through the Scriptures. So don't worry about what to say. Don't worry if nothing jumps out at you at first. God is patient. He will wait for the opportunity to get in. He will give you a word and lead you to understand its meaning for you today.

First reading: Listen

As you read the passage listen for a word or phrase that attracts you. Allow it to arise from the passage as if it is God's word for you today. Sit in silence repeating the word or phrase in your head.

Then say the word or phrase aloud.

Second reading: Ponder

As you read the passage again, ask how this word or phrase speaks to your life and why it has connected with you. Ponder it carefully. Don't worry if you get distracted – it may be part of your response to offer to God. Sit in silence and then frame a single sentence that begins to say aloud what this word or phrase says to you.

Third reading: Pray

As you read the passage for the last time, ask what Christ is calling from you. What is it that you need to do or consider or relinquish or take on as a result of what God is saying to you in this word or phrase? In the silence that follows the reading, pray for the grace of the Spirit to plant this word in your heart.

If you are in a group, talk for a few minutes and pray with each other.

If you are on your own, speak your prayer to God either aloud or in the silence of your heart.

If there is time, you may even want to read the passage a fourth time, and then end with the same silence before God with which you began.

+Stephen Cottrell

Monday 26 November

Psalms 92, **96** *or* **98**, 99, 101
Isaiah 40.1-11
Revelation 14.1-13

Revelation 14.1-13

'Fear God and give him glory' (v.7)

After the vision of the great beast in the previous chapter, the heavenly conqueror appears on Mount Zion. His appearance reveals in all its clarity the sharp division between those who have chosen to be faithful to Christ and those who have worshipped the beast. The 'two ways' of life and death are a familiar theme in scripture and in much Jewish and early Christian writing, but here they are set out in the starkest contrast. Salvation is not limited to the celibate martyrs who have already been redeemed. An angel brings the good news to those still on the earth, offering them the chance to recognize and respond to the true God. The invitation is quickly followed by further judgement as the downfall of 'Babylon' is announced. This is the persecuting Roman state that has so callously shed the blood of God's saints. The writer sees no glimmer of hope for those who have worshipped the beast.

Yet, in spite of this grim prophecy, a note of universalism is present. The eternal gospel of verse 6 is still offered to everyone on earth. Those who are facing death can be assured that they are not forgotten. They will rest from their labours, their trials over. The words of verse 13 have become familiar by being frequently used at funerals. The narrow vision of the Book of Revelation opens up to something universal in the experience of the Church.

COLLECT

Eternal Father,
whose Son Jesus Christ ascended to the throne of heaven
 that he might rule over all things as Lord and King:
keep the Church in the unity of the Spirit
and in the bond of peace,
and bring the whole created order to worship at his feet;
who is alive and reigns with you,
in the unity of the Holy Spirit,
one God, now and for ever.

10   *Reflection by* **Angela Tilby**

Psalms **97**, 98, 100 *or* **106*** (*or* 103) **Tuesday 27 November**
Isaiah 40.12-26
Revelation 14.14 – 15.end

Revelation 14.14 – 15.end

'Great and amazing are your deeds, Lord God, the Almighty!'
(15.3)

Two images of judgement dominate this passage: the harvesting of the earth and the seven bowls of the wrath of God. Between the two is a vision of the redeemed beside a sea of glass, mingled with fire. The scriptural allusions here come from the Exodus story. The song of the redeemed echoes that of the Israelites who have crossed the Red Sea, except that it contains the universal hope that all nations will come to worship the true God.

The problem for many of us in reflecting on this passage is the dominating theme of God's wrath. We could see this as a response to the history of bloodshed that has accompanied the human journey from time immemorial and still scars our world. God is not withdrawn from the horror of the world, but enters into it, experiencing it to the full through the suffering of Christ and his saints.

Vindictive as the theology of Revelation may seem, there is a countertheme of universal redemption. The wrath of God is not ultimate, but has an end. It may even, though with difficulty, be seen as therapeutic, for how can humanity be saved unless we are honest about our capacity for violence against our neighbours and ourselves? In all of this, the fire that cuts through the glassy sea recalls the Spirit, bringing life out of human chaos.

God the Father,
help us to hear the call of Christ the King
and to follow in his service,
whose kingdom has no end;
for he reigns with you and the Holy Spirit,
one God, one glory.

COLLECT

Reflection by **Angela Tilby**   11

Wednesday 28 November

Psalms 110, 111, **112**
or 110, **111**, 112
Isaiah 40.27 – 41.7
Revelation 16.1-11

Revelation 16.1-11

'You are just, O Holy One' (v.5)

The plagues poured out from the seven bowls of wrath remind us of the plagues of Egypt. Here, though, they are not intended to persuade Pharaoh to release God's people, but rather to demonstrate to the whole inhabited earth the extent of human wrongdoing. However, like the plagues of Egypt, they do not bring about a change of heart. Wounded as they are, the victims of the plagues do not repent but continue to curse God. It is as though the elements of creation have turned against humanity; the sea and the rivers turn to blood, the sun to scorching heat, and a deep darkness gathers over the kingdom of the beast. The justice of this judgement is underscored by the voice of the angel of the waters and the voice of the altar.

Although the detail of Revelation can be obscure and confusing, people have always resonated with its message of divine vengeance, perhaps because, in our hearts we long for justice and believe we deserve it. This is why, even in our age, we can see parallels between, for example, the damage human beings have done to our environment on earth, and the consequences this may yet have on our lives. The apocalyptic spirit is part of the human imagination and it is one way in which the living God speaks to us, warning us to change direction before it is too late.

COLLECT

Eternal Father,
whose Son Jesus Christ ascended to the throne of heaven
    that he might rule over all things as Lord and King:
keep the Church in the unity of the Spirit
and in the bond of peace,
and bring the whole created order to worship at his feet;
who is alive and reigns with you,
in the unity of the Holy Spirit,
one God, now and for ever.

| *Reflection by* **Angela Tilby**

Psalms **125**, 126, 127, 128
or 113, **115**
Isaiah 41.8-20
Revelation 16.12-end

Thursday 29 November

Revelation 16.12-end

'Blessed is the one who stays awake and is clothed' (v.15)

The sixth and seventh angels complete the outpouring of God's wrath. The consequence is the total break up of the physical geography and geology of the earth: the life-giving Euphrates dries up; the bowl flung into the air makes the mountains and islands vanish. The whole landscape is thus made strange and unfamiliar.

All this is the backdrop for the spirits of evil to make ready for the last and final battle at Armageddon, a location intended to recall Megiddo, where the righteous king Joshua met his fate. The demonic spirits preparing for battle are lying spirits, luring the bulk of humanity to destruction while the faithful remember the warnings of Jesus about the suddenness of his return (Matthew 24.43-4; I Thessalonians 5.2). They remain alert, clothed in holiness.

Armageddon has, of course, been a symbol of a final dramatic conflict through the whole of the Christian era. It has also come into modern times as an allusion to all-out global war – World War III to many of our contemporaries. It is not impossible that humanity might perish in a final nuclear conflagration, but it is doubtful that John foresaw this. His concern is, as always, the vindication of God's purpose and the certainty of judgment and redemption. This is what we hold on to in times of global threat.

God the Father,
help us to hear the call of Christ the King
and to follow in his service,
whose kingdom has no end;
for he reigns with you and the Holy Spirit,
one God, one glory.

COLLECT

Friday 30 November
Andrew the Apostle

Psalms 47, 147.1-12
Ezekiel 47.1-12
or Ecclesiasticus 14.20-end
John 12.20-32

Ezekiel 47.1-12

'... everything will live where the river goes' (v.9)

According to the Gospels, St Andrew was one of the first disciples to be called, a fisherman. Legend credits him with bringing the gospel to Georgia and other regions around the Black Sea.

Today's reading points to the life-giving power of God that gushes out from the temple sanctuary, bringing fertility to the land and life to the waters. The mission of the apostles is to bring life: knowledge of the living God, dignity to the human person, energy and purpose to the human community. The Christian life is about much more than religion, though at its heart is the thirst for holiness. The energy of God's life is unstoppable. The water flows from the sanctuary whether or not it is adequately channelled by human beings; it is 'deep enough to swim in', and eventually so deep that it cannot be crossed. The gospel is for everyone; the fish produced by the river are 'of a great many kinds'. This passage has perhaps influenced the account of the fishing miracle in John's Gospel (John 21.11) and suggests that God desires his image to be brought to fulfilment in many and diverse ways.

Apostles are missionaries, and we share their calling to be caught up in the living stream of God's love for the world. We can never control or determine the path of that stream, but we can – and should – go with its flow.

COLLECT

Almighty God,
who gave such grace to your apostle Saint Andrew
that he readily obeyed the call of your Son Jesus Christ
    and brought his brother with him:
call us by your holy word,
and give us grace to follow you without delay
    and to tell the good news of your kingdom;
through Jesus Christ your Son our Lord,
who is alive and reigns with you,
in the unity of the Holy Spirit,
one God, now and for ever.

Reflection by **Angela Tilby**

Psalms **145** *or* 120, **121**, 122   **Saturday 1 December**
Isaiah 42.10-17
Revelation 18

Revelation 18

'Come out of her, my people' (v.4)

This great denunciation of 'Babylon', Rome, foresees the destruction of the great city as though it were happening at the present moment. Rome is guilty of the blood of the martyrs; her basic sin is idolatry, which includes the worship of the emperor. The destruction is total. All the wealth that has flooded into the city from other parts of the empire is finished. In fact, of course, John's prophecy and vision were unfulfilled. Rome did not fall in the early Christian era. Even more surprisingly, with the conversion of Constantine, Christianity became the faith of the Roman Empire.

There are two points at which the prophecy of Rome's downfall has something to say to us. The first is to note that the denunciation includes judgements that Jesus himself made against Jerusalem; compare verse 24 with Matthew 23.34-37a ('Jerusalem, Jerusalem, the city that kills the prophets and stones those who are sent to it!', v.37). A city that kills God's prophets is always going to come under God's judgement.

The second point is that there is a call to God's people to detach themselves from the corruption of the city, including its tendency to worship wealth and power. Christians should always be alert to the temptation to covetousness and avarice. Prosperous cities can be built on brutal injustice, and the Christian community of Rome is warned, as we are, not to be seduced by the city's false glamour.

Eternal Father,
whose Son Jesus Christ ascended to the throne of heaven
that he might rule over all things as Lord and King:
keep the Church in the unity of the Spirit
and in the bond of peace,
and bring the whole created order to worship at his feet;
who is alive and reigns with you,
in the unity of the Holy Spirit,
one God, now and for ever.

COLLECT

Reflection by **Angela Tilby**   15

Monday 3 December

Psalms **50**, 54 *or* **1**, 2, 3
Isaiah 42.18-end
Revelation 19

Revelation 19

'Hallelujah! For the Lord our God the Almighty reigns' (v.6)

The book of Revelation is full of songs, and these words (or their King James equivalent) are from the most famous song of all, set by Handel in his oratorio *Messiah*. What is striking is that all the songs in the book come *before* the great battles with the beast (vv.19-20) and the dragon, or Satan (Revelation 20.2-3). Is this complacency – pious Christians trying to airbrush their problems away? No – and neither is it premature. It is praise, and in the Bible, especially in books such as Daniel and Revelation, praise is not the same as thanksgiving. Praise means lifting God's future into the present and celebrating it *as though it were happening now*.

Cleric and political activist Allan Boesak, writing about the songs of praise in the book of Revelation during the apartheid years in South Africa, understood this perfectly: 'Oppressed people in South Africa understand the need for singing ... And besides, it drives the dragon crazy when you sing about his downfall even though you are bleeding.'

Advent is supremely the time to shake off any apathetic feeling that we can do nothing to change the world. We can: we can sing a better one into being, and the praise songs of Revelation make an excellent place to start.

COLLECT

Almighty God,
give us grace to cast away the works of darkness
and to put on the armour of light,
now in the time of this mortal life,
in which your Son Jesus Christ came to us in great humility;
that on the last day,
when he shall come again in his glorious majesty
    to judge the living and the dead,
we may rise to the life immortal;
through him who is alive and reigns with you,
in the unity of the Holy Spirit,
one God, now and for ever.

16   *Reflection by* **Gordon Mursell**

Psalms **80**, 82 *or* **5**, 6 (8)   **Tuesday 4 December**
Isaiah 43.1-13
Revelation 20

Revelation 20

*'... they will be priests of God and of Christ, and they will reign
with him for a thousand years' (v.6)*

With these words, the writer of Revelation describes the Millennium,
the thousand-year reign of Christ on earth before the final
consummation of all things. Like everything in Revelation, it is a
striking mix of this world and the next, a vision of all creation
transfigured. But it begins here and now, with the transformation
of the present world order into the realm of Christ the King.
Furthermore, Christians will have a crucial role to play, as priests and
kings. They will be priestly because they will share Christ's work of
mediating between heaven and earth, reconciling each to the other,
and because they will be there *for others*, not just for themselves.
They will be royal because they will *matter* – and for all eternity – as
sharers in the life and victory of Christ.

In this tremendous vision, no one will be unemployed, and no one
will be preoccupied with self. At the heart of the vision stands a great
throne, and on it will sit Someone greater than all the leaders of this
world. But that Someone has the appearance and character of a
lamb, whose self-offering opens the way to an upside-down creation
in which the powerful will be brought low and the humble lifted
high. Here, surely, is a vision of the future that is worth praying and
striving for now.

Almighty God,
as your kingdom dawns,
turn us from the darkness of sin to the
light of holiness,
that we may be ready to meet you
in our Lord and Saviour, Jesus Christ.

COLLECT

Reflection by **Gordon Mursell**   17

Wednesday 5 December

Revelation 21.1-8

*'And the one who was seated on the throne said,
"See, I am making all things new"' (21.5)*

The Greek word for 'new' comes four times in these few verses: a new heaven, a new earth, the new Jerusalem, and finally 'I am making all things new'. The vision we are given here is nothing less than a new creation, with three distinctive features: first, there will be no more sea, because the old creation was made out of the watery chaos (Genesis 1.2) and was always liable to return to it, as it did in the days of Noah. No insularity in the new creation!

Second, there will be no more death, or mourning or crying, or pain – these tragic flaws in the old creation will be banished for ever from the new one.

Third, God will be with us; in fact, God's 'tent' or tabernacle will be pitched among us for ever. We will become in reality what we have always been in potential: God's children.

This, and nothing less than this, is what the Christian is to look forward to, and to begin to build here and now. The first citizens of this new creation will be precisely those who have grieved and wept and suffered the most in the old one; they will enjoy the front seats at a banquet at which the best wine is still to be served.

COLLECT

Almighty God,
give us grace to cast away the works of darkness
and to put on the armour of light,
now in the time of this mortal life,
in which your Son Jesus Christ came to us in great humility;
that on the last day,
when he shall come again in his glorious majesty
    to judge the living and the dead,
we may rise to the life immortal;
through him who is alive and reigns with you,
in the unity of the Holy Spirit,
one God, now and for ever.

Reflection by **Gordon Mursell**

Psalms **42**, 43 *or* 14, **15**, 16
Isaiah 44.1-8
Revelation 21.9-21

Thursday 6 December

Revelation 21.9-21

'... he showed me the holy city Jerusalem coming down out of heaven from God' (21.10)

There is a striking paradox at the heart of the Bible's closing vision of the new Jerusalem. It will have 'a great, high wall with twelve gates'. But (as we see in tomorrow's reading) the gates will never be shut. It will be a safe place, a refuge, which is why nothing unclean or evil will be found there. It will also be an inclusive place: we may be surprised at who turn out to be our fellow-citizens, and they may be surprised to see us!

More important still: it will be a *beautiful* place, transparent as glass; the precious stones and jewels that here are the privilege of the few will there be the delight of the many. In the New Testament, the Greek word for 'good' (*kalos*) also means 'beautiful', and that matters, because surely our greatest challenge in the twenty-first century is how to give birth to a vision of goodness that is not just about the absence of evil, but is truly attractive in its own right.

Well, here is that vision: a safe, inclusive and beautiful city where only those who freely choose a lifestyle and ideology hostile to its values will exclude themselves. Advent is the season to pray that vision into reality. Charles Wesley gave us the words:

Come, thou long-expected Jesus,
Born to set thy people free,
From our fears and sins release us,
Let us find our rest in thee.

Almighty God,
as your kingdom dawns,
turn us from the darkness of sin to the
light of holiness,
that we may be ready to meet you
in our Lord and Saviour, Jesus Christ.

COLLECT

Reflection by **Gordon Mursell** | 19

Friday 7 December

Psalms **25**, 26 *or* 17, **19**
Isaiah 44.9-23
Revelation 21.22 – 22.5

Revelation 21.22 – 22.5

*'Then the angel showed me the river of the water of life,
bright as crystal' (22.1)*

The vision of the city with which the Bible ends is not the same as the Garden of Eden with which it begins, but they do have much in common. Eden is a paradise garden, and the first man and woman are commanded 'to till it and keep it' (Genesis 2.15) – nature and human culture belonged together in the presence of God, before everything went wrong. In the new Jerusalem, nature and human culture will be perfectly integrated: the tree of life, with its fruit and leaves 'for the healing of the nations', and the river that flows through the city, will be complemented by 'the glory and the honour of the nations'. No temple will be needed: everyone will enjoy direct access to the presence of God.

This tremendous vision of a creation made new comes *from exile* (Revelation 1.9). In our world today, borders and barriers are increasingly closed against refugees, asylum seekers and others forced into exile. Yet the Bible suggests that those excluded may be precisely the ones capable of envisioning, and helping us build, a new and better world.

Advent is the time to ask: what can we do to develop a vision of that new world, and who are the people who can help us to build it?

COLLECT

Almighty God,
give us grace to cast away the works of darkness
and to put on the armour of light,
now in the time of this mortal life,
in which your Son Jesus Christ came to us in great humility;
that on the last day,
when he shall come again in his glorious majesty
    to judge the living and the dead,
we may rise to the life immortal;
through him who is alive and reigns with you,
in the unity of the Holy Spirit,
one God, now and for ever.

Reflection by **Gordon Mursell**

Psalms **9**, (10) *or* 20, 21, **23**
Isaiah 44.24 – 45.13
Revelation 22.6-end

Revelation 22.6-end

'Amen. Come, Lord Jesus!' (v.20)

The Greek verb 'to come' appears seven times in these closing verses of Revelation, just as it appears three times in the opening verses. In his wonderful Advent hymn, based directly on texts from Revelation, Charles Wesley captures this emphasis on a God who comes: 'Lo! He comes with clouds descending' echoes Revelation 1.7 ('Behold, he cometh with clouds' in the KJV), and his closing line, 'Alleluia! Come, Lord, come!' echoes verse 20 of this chapter. The whole hymn, like the book, is focused on the need for expectant, even defiant, waiting for the God who comes among us – at Christmas, in the word made flesh; at the end of time, as our Judge; and every day, wherever and whenever people have hearts and minds ready to make that God welcome.

Like any good preacher, Wesley follows John of Patmos in verse 20 by moving from testimony (talking *about* God, in the first three verses of his hymn) to prayer (talking *to* God) in the closing verse. It is sad that, in his equally famous Christmas hymn ('Hark! The herald angels sing'), the closing verse, where he again moves from talking about God to talking to God, is invariably omitted today, for it is precisely in these closing words that we are invited to make the message of Scripture our own, and open our hearts to the God who comes:

Come, Desire of nations, come,
Fix in us thy humble home...

Almighty God,
as your kingdom dawns,
turn us from the darkness of sin to the
light of holiness,
that we may be ready to meet you
in our Lord and Saviour, Jesus Christ.

COLLECT

Monday 10 December

1 Thessalonians 1

'For the people of those regions report ... how you turned to God from idols, to serve a living and true God, and to wait for his Son from heaven' (vv.9-10)

These words give us a fascinating insight into how members of one of the very earliest churches became Christians, and the three stages involved in doing this. First, they 'turned to God from idols' – the verb 'turn' occurs rarely in Paul's letters and always involves some kind of change of life and direction. There were plenty of idols for those first Christians to turn from (including the growing cult of emperor worship), and there are plenty today.

Second, they turned in order 'to serve a living and true God'. At the heart of Christian life is this costly willingness to put self second, and service of God and neighbour first.

Third, they committed themselves 'to wait for his Son from heaven'. The Greek word for 'wait' occurs nowhere else in the New Testament, and has about it a sense of hanging on in there (it comes from a root meaning 'abide').

Here is the spirituality of Advent: what idols do we need to turn from? What service of God and neighbour do we need to commit to? And are we waiting expectantly for what God longs to do in our lives today?

COLLECT

O Lord, raise up, we pray, your power
and come among us,
and with great might succour us;
that whereas, through our sins and wickedness
we are grievously hindered
in running the race that is set before us,
your bountiful grace and mercy
may speedily help and deliver us;
through Jesus Christ your Son our Lord,
to whom with you and the Holy Spirit,
be honour and glory, now and for ever.

Reflection by **Gordon Mursell**

Tuesday 11 December

1 Thessalonians 2.1-12

'But we were gentle among you, like a nurse tenderly caring for her own children' (v.7)

The image of the apostle as a nurse caring for her own children is striking, and not only because it complements the more traditional image of the apostle 'like a father with his children' that follows it. The image carries overtones of feeding and nurturing, just as the Greek word for 'tenderly caring' carries overtones of keeping warm.

Two implications of the apostle as nurse are worth noting. First, Paul sees the vocation of an apostle as far more than dispensing professional skills – it involves ministering with one's own self, making oneself vulnerable to rejection. This makes Christian pastoral care costly; it also makes it potentially life changing. Second, the nurse does not care for her dependent children indefinitely; there will come a time to let them go, even though the nurse will never cease to care about them.

What this nurse offers her children is nothing less than unconditional love, which is why Paul goes on to speak of sharing his own self with the Thessalonian Christians, 'because you have become very dear to us'. Above all, Paul wants those Christians to know that they are loved, and his ministry as a nurse embodies the love that God shows to all of us at Christmas by becoming human among us.

Almighty God,
purify our hearts and minds,
that when your Son Jesus Christ comes again as
judge and saviour
we may be ready to receive him,
who is our Lord and our God.

COLLECT

Reflection by **Gordon Mursell** 23

Wednesday 12 December

1 Thessalonians 2.13-end

'…but Satan blocked our way' (v.18)

Suddenly, Paul's letter to the Thessalonians is overshadowed by evil. The best-laid plans of even the greatest Christian apostle are unexpectedly thwarted – and by Satan. We need to be careful here: there is no suggestion that Paul attributes all or most of human sin and suffering to the work of a personal devil, turning us into helpless pawns in an epic cosmic battle. But the Bible does suggest that evil is a real and active force in the world, which, like cancer, can take over entire people and organizations if not confronted and challenged.

Advent is supremely the season to remember that. The beauty of the Christmas story is stained by Herod's terrible massacre of the Innocents. And we are told in the Gospel of John that Satan entered into Judas Iscariot, not when he was conspiring with others to betray Jesus but right in the middle of the Last Supper (John 13.27).

It's easy, and tempting, to view Herod or Judas as embodiments of pure evil; it would be wiser to admit that in any situation, no matter how spiritual, human frailty is exposed to the reality of evil. Rigorous and vigilant self-examination are essential here. In an Advent sermon, John Henry Newman wrote: 'we are destined to come before Him; nay, and to come before Him in judgment; and that on our first meeting; and that suddenly.'

COLLECT

O Lord, raise up, we pray, your power
and come among us,
and with great might succour us;
that whereas, through our sins and wickedness
we are grievously hindered
in running the race that is set before us,
your bountiful grace and mercy
may speedily help and deliver us;
through Jesus Christ your Son our Lord,
to whom with you and the Holy Spirit,
be honour and glory, now and for ever.

24   *Reflection by* **Gordon Mursell**

Psalms 53, **54**, 60 *or* **37***
Isaiah 48.1-11
1 Thessalonians 3

Thursday 13 December

1 Thessalonians 3

'And may the Lord make you ... abound in love for one another and for all, just as we abound in love for you' (v.12)

If (as many scholars argue) St Paul's first letter to the Thessalonians is the earliest piece of writing in the New Testament, then verses 11 to 13 of chapter 3 form the earliest Christian prayer in written form. Notice that it comes in the middle of the letter: Paul has no difficulty moving from pastoral encouragement to prayer and back again, rather than (as can sometimes happen today) cordoning prayer off from the rest of Church life by restricting it to the beginning and end of a meeting or other activity.

Paul's prayer for God to strengthen their hearts in holiness so that they may be blameless 'at the coming of our Lord Jesus' captures exactly what we might call the spirituality of Advent. What is even more striking is his prayer for them to abound in love for one another and for all. From the very beginning, Christians were to be concerned with all humanity, not just a chosen few; hence the writer of 1 Timothy urges the recipient to pray 'for everyone ... in the sight of God our Saviour, who desires everyone to be saved' (1 Timothy 2.1-4).

Advent is a time to enlarge the focus of our prayer and witness to embrace nothing less than the whole of creation.

Almighty God,
purify our hearts and minds,
that when your Son Jesus Christ comes again as
judge and saviour
we may be ready to receive him,
who is our Lord and our God.

COLLECT

Reflection by **Gordon Mursell** | 25

Friday 14 December

1 Thessalonians 4.1-12

'... you yourselves have been taught by God to love one another'
(v.9)

The first letter to the Thessalonians gives us a fascinating picture of a young and fragile Christian community struggling to survive and grow against a background of what seems to have been a mix of indifference and active hostility. Paul speaks in this chapter about the 'lustful passion' of the gentiles, and earlier he writes about adherents of Judaism who 'drove us out' (1 Thessalonians 2.15; Bishop Tom Wright helpfully suggests that they should be described as 'Judeans' rather than 'Jews', since all the earliest Christians were Jews, including Paul himself).

Paul wants those first Christians to stand out by their love for one another. But many good Judeans and pagans will also have loved one another. What surely made the followers of Jesus distinctive was their assurance that they were themselves unconditionally loved (Paul calls them 'beloved by God', 1 Thessalonians 1.4), irrespective of whether they were Jews or gentiles in origin. This is the unique gift and the living heart of Christian faith: that all people, whatever our upbringing, orientation or ethnicity, can come to know that we are loved with the love that is made flesh in the incarnation and crucifixion of God's only Son, and which should find living and outgoing expression in the life of the Church.

COLLECT

O Lord, raise up, we pray, your power
and come among us,
and with great might succour us;
that whereas, through our sins and wickedness
we are grievously hindered
in running the race that is set before us,
your bountiful grace and mercy
may speedily help and deliver us;
through Jesus Christ your Son our Lord,
to whom with you and the Holy Spirit,
be honour and glory, now and for ever.

Reflection by **Gordon Mursell**

Psalms **145** *or* 41, **42**, 43
Isaiah 49.1-13
1 Thessalonians 4.13-end

Saturday 15 December

1 Thessalonians 4.13-end

'For the Lord himself, with a cry of command … will descend from heaven' (v.16)

With these dramatic words, Paul seeks to reassure the Thessalonian Christians, who were evidently anxious that those of their number who had already died would miss out on the resurrection, by contrast with those who were still alive at Christ's second coming. This may not be a major concern for us today, but what Paul writes remains of enduring importance. Those who have died 'in Christ' will be the first to experience the fullness of resurrection life.

Paul doesn't specify what it means to be 'in Christ', or whether this includes righteous non-believers. What he does say is that we will be reunited with those we love but see no longer, and that, like the father of the Prodigal Son, the risen Christ will already be on the road, so to speak, to meet us and bring us home.

What's more, we will *hear* his coming ('with a cry of command, with the archangel's call and with the sound of God's trumpet'). In Scripture, hearing is always the primary sense, and Advent is the season for attuning our ears so we can hear, as Mary and Zechariah both did, the call of God into a new and life-changing future. If we can hear God's call to us now, then God's final call at the end of time will be nothing less than a welcome home.

Almighty God,
purify our hearts and minds,
that when your Son Jesus Christ comes again as
judge and saviour
we may be ready to receive him,
who is our Lord and our God.

COLLECT

Reflection by **Gordon Mursell**

27

Monday 17 December

Psalm **40** *or* **44**
Isaiah 49.14-25
1 Thessalonians 5.1-11

1 Thessalonians 5.1-11

'For God has destined us not for wrath ...' (v.9)

In the 1970s, when there were serious troubles in Northern Ireland, Dr Ian Paisley became the most prominent – and belligerent – of the Protestant leaders. The Prime Minister, James Callaghan, once said to him, 'We are all children of God, are we not?' 'No,' Paisley thundered, 'we are children of wrath.'

In Ephesians 2.3 Paul says of himself and his fellow Christians, 'we were by nature children of wrath, like everyone else'. But writing to the Thessalonians, Paul tells them that their faith means they are destined 'not for wrath' but for 'salvation through our Lord Jesus Christ'.

There is an innate tendency in human beings to do the wrong thing even when we desire to do what is right. Paul could wax eloquently about it. We call it original sin, and it is now a very unfashionable concept in the western world. It is what has led many people to believe they are under condemnation and subject to God's wrath. But the most grievous judges of human beings are frequently human beings themselves. Even in an age that scarcely believes in sin, wrath and hell, many people remain deeply dissatisfied with their lives and with themselves. A saviour is still needed. Jesus Christ looks upon us not as captive to the evil one but as liberated by his saving love. That's why we can claim truly to be children of God.

COLLECT

O Lord Jesus Christ,
who at your first coming sent your messenger
to prepare your way before you:
grant that the ministers and stewards of your mysteries
may likewise so prepare and make ready your way
by turning the hearts of the disobedient to the wisdom of the just,
that at your second coming to judge the world
we may be found an acceptable people in your sight;
for you are alive and reign with the Father
in the unity of the Holy Spirit,
one God, now and for ever.

Reflection by **Graham James**

Psalms **70**, 74 *or* **48**, 52
Isaiah 50
1 Thessalonians 5.12-end

Tuesday 18 December

1 Thessalonians 5.12-end

'... encourage the faint-hearted, help the weak' (v.14)

The Greek word translated here as 'faint-hearted' makes its only appearance in the whole of the New Testament in this letter from Paul to the Thessalonians. A literal translation would be 'little-souled'. 'Faint-hearted', if used at all in English now, would be likely to refer to people who are nervous, anxious and afraid, passing through life in a permanent state of underconfidence. But Paul seems to be thinking of the diffident people in the Thessalonian congregation, the ones who don't place much value on themselves or think they have little to offer. That's why they're described as 'little-souled'.

In Greek culture, someone with lots of self-confidence and self-assurance was thought to be a 'great-souled' person. Such people were endowed, it was believed, with qualities of leadership. Yet it may well be the diffident and modest who have much more of the meekness and humility that Jesus said in the Sermon on the Mount would cause them to inherit the earth. The contemporary world is as liable to admire the 'great-souled' self-confident leader as ancient Greece. As Christmas approaches and we celebrate God coming to earth in the defenceless humility of a newborn baby, perhaps we should spare a thought for the faint-hearted, diffident and humble people in congregations everywhere. They are often the ones most ready to serve. They should be encouraged to believe they have greater souls than they think.

COLLECT

God for whom we watch and wait,
you sent John the Baptist to prepare the way of your Son:
give us courage to speak the truth,
to hunger for justice,
and to suffer for the cause of right,
with Jesus Christ our Lord.

Reflection by **Graham James**

Wednesday 19 December

2 Thessalonians 1

'... we ... boast of you among the churches of God' (v.4)

One of Aesop's fables is about a boastful traveller. He claims that when staying in Rhodes many people witnessed him leaping further than any other human being. A bystander asks him to pretend it is Rhodes and repeat his feat. It put an end to his boasting.

In the contemporary world, boasting seems almost compulsory. Some job applications or curriculum vitae I read make me feel rather inferior to the possessors of such great talents. Yet when I meet such people in the flesh they are frequently far from boastful. In their applications for jobs they are simply doing what the culture requires.

Sometimes in his letters, Paul boasts ironically of his sufferings, imprisonments and persecutions, the signs that he's an authentic apostle of Jesus Christ (2 Corinthians 10.12). In this letter he isn't boasting about himself or his achievements but the faith and perseverance of the Thessalonians, a young church facing persecution. We don't know the precise circumstances, but what impresses Paul is their love for each other and refusal to abandon Christ despite the pressure put upon them. He tells the Thessalonians he boasts of their story to other churches to encourage them.

Many churches across the world are experiencing persecution in our own age, notably in Egypt and Pakistan, Syria and elsewhere in the Middle East. Do we even know the extent of their sufferings? Do we boast of them enough?

C O L L E C T

O Lord Jesus Christ,
who at your first coming sent your messenger
to prepare your way before you:
grant that the ministers and stewards of your mysteries
may likewise so prepare and make ready your way
by turning the hearts of the disobedient to the wisdom of the just,
that at your second coming to judge the world
we may be found an acceptable people in your sight;
for you are alive and reign with the Father
in the unity of the Holy Spirit,
one God, now and for ever.

Reflection by **Graham James**

Psalms **46**, 95
Isaiah 51.9-16
2 Thessalonians 2

Thursday 20 December

2 Thessalonians 2

'Let no one deceive you in any way...' (v.3)

One of the members of the nonconformist church I attended in my childhood believed strongly that the end times were imminent. He distributed tracts and preached at street corners. Sadly, he had a very unsmiling countenance and carried with him a deep gloom.

The Thessalonians to whom Paul writes believed the end times were imminent too. They were much more cheerful about it, though. For them, the world had been so recently turned upside down by the resurrection of Christ and the coming of the Holy Spirit that they thought God would surely bring things to completion very soon. Some of them even believed the day of the Lord had already come. The gifts of the Spirit were such that miraculous things were happening. Lives were being changed. Surely that was what was promised when Christ would return?

Paul is concerned that they should not be deceived. But it's hard not to have some sympathy with the Thessalonians. When lives are so transformed in Christ that people have become a new creation, doesn't it seem like an anticipation of the 'day of the Lord'?

Two thousand years of Christian history have dulled such expectation. The Christian Church has long been an established institution. Yet we still live in an interim time between Pentecost and the second coming of Christ, however we may understand it. A touch of Thessalonian excitement might do us all some good.

God for whom we watch and wait,
you sent John the Baptist to prepare the way of your Son:
give us courage to speak the truth,
to hunger for justice,
and to suffer for the cause of right,
with Jesus Christ our Lord.

COLLECT

Reflection by **Graham James**   31

Friday 21 December

2 Thessalonians 3

'I, Paul, write this greeting with my own hand' (v.17)

Paul sometimes finishes his letters with a greeting in his own handwriting to authenticate them. It was common in the ancient world for letter writers (Cicero comes to mind) to dictate them to a scribe and then add a personal greeting of their own at the end. Here Paul seems almost to overdo it, saying 'this is the mark in every letter of mine; it is the way I write'.

A handwritten letter has now become something of a rarity in the western world. Yet it is often the more precious as a result. A bereaved person will read letters of condolence again and again. Phone calls don't have the same permanence. 'Thank you for writing in your own hand,' I've been told at such times. Electronic communication cannot be cherished in quite the same way.

In 2016 the Bishop's Art Prize in Norwich (a competition I sponsor each year at the Norwich University of the Arts) was won by a bronze simply called *Epistle*. It was cast from a pile of handwritten letters, given weight and permanence, a sign of how much they meant to the people who received them.

The weight the Church has given to Paul's letters as scripture may cause us to forget just how personal they were for those who first read them. Do we write enough letters in our own hand? When and to whom should we write them?

COLLECT

O Lord Jesus Christ,
who at your first coming sent your messenger
to prepare your way before you:
grant that the ministers and stewards of your mysteries
may likewise so prepare and make ready your way
by turning the hearts of the disobedient to the wisdom of the just,
that at your second coming to judge the world
we may be found an acceptable people in your sight;
for you are alive and reign with the Father
in the unity of the Holy Spirit,
one God, now and for ever.

| *Reflection by* **Graham James**

Saturday 22 December

Isaiah 52.1-12

'How beautiful ... are the feet ...' (v.7)

It's estimated that in an average life span most people will walk 20,000 miles, and frequently a great deal more than that. It's the rough equivalent of walking round the world. Our feet have a lot of work to do, though we tend to take them for granted. That's why this verse in Isaiah is such an arresting and intriguing one.

Our feet can be a mirror to our general health. Problems with the circulation of our blood as well as signs of arthritis or diabetes may be detected first in our feet. But we don't generally regard our feet as the most attractive part of the human body.

The word in Hebrew, *na'ha*, which we translate as 'beautiful' does not mean pretty or alluring. It's more to do with being appropriate and fitting, entirely aligned with God's purpose. So feet are beautiful when they do the right work, God's work. Here it's the feet of heralds that are beautiful because they are proclaiming a message of freedom for the people of Israel, announcing their homecoming.

In Romans 10.15, Paul takes this verse and applies it to those who are sent into the world to preach the gospel. The good news of Jesus Christ has been carried on foot to every part of the globe in Christian mission. Where will our feet take us today and for what purpose?

God for whom we watch and wait,
you sent John the Baptist to prepare the way of your Son:
give us courage to speak the truth,
to hunger for justice,
and to suffer for the cause of right,
with Jesus Christ our Lord.

COLLECT

Reflection by **Graham James**

Monday 24 December

Christmas Eve

Isaiah 52.13 – end of 53

'... we held him of no account' (53.3)

Isaiah's vision of the suffering servant 'wounded for our transgressions, crushed for our iniquities' seems a natural reading for Good Friday. So it's something of a surprise when it appears on Christmas Eve, read in churches already festooned with Christmas trees, their cribs set up awaiting only the addition of the child in the manger.

Among the things that unite Christmas Eve and Good Friday is the indifference of the local population, whether to the birth of Jesus in Bethlehem or to his crucifixion in Jerusalem. A few shepherds apart, Bethlehem 'held him of no account'. Only later, after the visit of Eastern sages, did Herod fear for his kingdom and try to trace this special child. On the eve of Christ's birth, his parents were homeless travellers, also of no account. On Good Friday in Jerusalem, his mother Mary and a few others were at the foot of the cross, but the life of the city was barely interrupted by yet another felon going to his execution. The central events of Christianity took place largely unnoticed by the world.

More people go to church in England nowadays on Christmas Eve than on any other day of the year. Perhaps it's especially at Christmas, when suddenly what the Church offers becomes popular, we need to recall not just the harsh circumstances of Christ's birth but remember the world at the time 'held him of no account', both at his birth and death.

COLLECT

Almighty God,
you make us glad with the yearly remembrance
    of the birth of your Son Jesus Christ:
grant that, as we joyfully receive him as our redeemer,
so we may with sure confidence behold him
when he shall come to be our judge;
who is alive and reigns with you,
in the unity of the Holy Spirit,
one God, now and for ever.

| *Reflection by* **Graham James**

Morning Prayer – a simple form

Preparation

O Lord, open our lips
and our mouth shall proclaim your praise.

A prayer of thanksgiving for Advent

Blessed are you, Sovereign God of all,
to you be praise and glory for ever.
In your tender compassion
the dawn from on high is breaking upon us
to dispel the lingering shadows of night.
As we look for your coming among us this day,
open our eyes to behold your presence
and strengthen our hands to do your will,
that the world may rejoice and give you praise.
Blessed be God, Father, Son and Holy Spirit.
Blessed be God for ever.

Word of God

Psalmody *(the psalm or psalms listed for the day)*

Glory to the Father and to the Son
and to the Holy Spirit;
as it was in the beginning is now:
and shall be for ever. Amen.

Reading from Holy Scripture *(one or both of the passages set for the day)*

Reflection

The Benedictus (The Song of Zechariah) *(see opposite page)*

Prayers

Intercessions – a time of prayer for the day and its tasks, the world and its need, the church and her life.

The Collect for the Day

The Lord's Prayer *(see p. 38)*

Conclusion

A blessing or the Grace *(see p. 38)*, or a concluding response

Let us bless the Lord
Thanks be to God

35

Benedictus (The Song of Zechariah)

1 Blessed be the Lord the God of Israel, ♦
    who has come to his people and set them free.

2 He has raised up for us a mighty Saviour, ♦
    born of the house of his servant David.

3 Through his holy prophets God promised of old ♦
    to save us from our enemies,
        from the hands of all that hate us,

4 To show mercy to our ancestors, ♦
    and to remember his holy covenant.

5 This was the oath God swore to our father Abraham: ♦
    to set us free from the hands of our enemies,

6 Free to worship him without fear, ♦
    holy and righteous in his sight
        all the days of our life.

7 And you, child, shall be called the prophet of the Most High, ♦
    for you will go before the Lord to prepare his way,

8 To give his people knowledge of salvation ♦
    by the forgiveness of all their sins.

9 In the tender compassion of our God ♦
    the dawn from on high shall break upon us,

10 To shine on those who dwell in darkness
        and the shadow of death, ♦
    and to guide our feet into the way of peace.

Luke 1.68-79

**Glory to the Father and to the Son
and to the Holy Spirit;
as it was in the beginning is now:
and shall be for ever. Amen.**

Seasonal Prayers of Thanksgiving

Advent

Blessed are you, Sovereign God of all,
to you be praise and glory for ever.
In your tender compassion
the dawn from on high is breaking upon us
to dispel the lingering shadows of night.
As we look for your coming among us this day,
open our eyes to behold your presence
and strengthen our hands to do your will,
that the world may rejoice and give you praise.
Blessed be God, Father, Son and Holy Spirit.
Blessed be God for ever.

At Any Time

Blessed are you, creator of all,
to you be praise and glory for ever.
As your dawn renews the face of the earth
bringing light and life to all creation,
may we rejoice in this day you have made;
as we wake refreshed from the depths of sleep,
open our eyes to behold your presence
and strengthen our hands to do your will,
that the world may rejoice and give you praise.
Blessed be God, Father, Son and Holy Spirit.
Blessed be God for ever.

after Lancelot Andrewes (1626)

The Lord's Prayer and The Grace

Our Father in heaven,
hallowed be your name,
your kingdom come,
your will be done,
on earth as in heaven.
Give us today our daily bread.
Forgive us our sins
as we forgive those who sin against us.
Lead us not into temptation
but deliver us from evil.
For the kingdom, the power,
and the glory are yours
now and for ever.
Amen.

(or)

Our Father, who art in heaven,
hallowed be thy name;
thy kingdom come;
thy will be done;
on earth as it is in heaven.
Give us this day our daily bread.
And forgive us our trespasses,
as we forgive those who trespass against us.
And lead us not into temptation;
but deliver us from evil.
For thine is the kingdom,
the power and the glory,
for ever and ever.
Amen.

The grace of our Lord Jesus Christ,
and the love of God,
and the fellowship of the Holy Spirit,
be with us all evermore.
Amen.

An Order for Night Prayer (Compline)

The Lord almighty grant us a quiet night and a perfect end.
Amen.

Our help is in the name of the Lord
who made heaven and earth.

A period of silence for reflection on the past day may follow.

The following or other suitable words of penitence may be used

Most merciful God,
we confess to you,
before the whole company of heaven and one another,
that we have sinned in thought, word and deed
and in what we have failed to do.
Forgive us our sins,
heal us by your Spirit
and raise us to new life in Christ. Amen.

O God, make speed to save us.
O Lord, make haste to help us.

Glory to the Father and to the Son
and to the Holy Spirit;
as it was in the beginning is now
and shall be for ever. Amen.
Alleluia.

The following or another suitable hymn may be sung

Before the ending of the day,
Creator of the world, we pray
That you, with steadfast love, would keep
Your watch around us while we sleep.

From evil dreams defend our sight,
From fears and terrors of the night;
Tread underfoot our deadly foe
That we no sinful thought may know.

O Father, that we ask be done
Through Jesus Christ, your only Son;
And Holy Spirit, by whose breath
Our souls are raised to life from death.

The Word of God

Psalmody

One or more of Psalms 4, 91 or 134 may be used.

Psalm 134

1   Come, bless the Lord, all you servants of the Lord, ♦
you that by night stand in the house of the Lord.

2   Lift up your hands towards the sanctuary ♦
and bless the Lord.

3   The Lord who made heaven and earth ♦
give you blessing out of Zion.

**Glory to the Father and to the Son
and to the Holy Spirit;
as it was in the beginning is now
and shall be for ever. Amen.**

Scripture Reading

*One of the following short lessons or another suitable
passage is read*

You, O Lord, are in the midst of us and we are called by your
name; leave us not, O Lord our God.

Jeremiah 14.9

(or)

Be sober, be vigilant, because your adversary the devil is
prowling round like a roaring lion, seeking for someone
to devour. Resist him, strong in the faith.

1 Peter 5.8,9

(or)

The servants of the Lamb shall see the face of God, whose name
will be on their foreheads. There will be no more night: they will
not need the light of a lamp or the light of the sun, for God will
be their light, and they will reign for ever and ever.

Revelation 22.4,5

Into your hands, O Lord, I commend my spirit.
Into your hands, O Lord, I commend my spirit.
For you have redeemed me, Lord God of truth.
I commend my spirit.
Glory to the Father and to the Son
and to the Holy Spirit.
Into your hands, O Lord, I commend my spirit.

Or, in Easter

Into your hands, O Lord, I commend my spirit.
    Alleluia, alleluia.
Into your hands, O Lord, I commend my spirit.
    Alleluia, alleluia.
For you have redeemed me, Lord God of truth.
Alleluia, alleluia.
Glory to the Father and to the Son
and to the Holy Spirit.
Into your hands, O Lord, I commend my spirit.
    Alleluia, alleluia.

Keep me as the apple of your eye.
Hide me under the shadow of your wings.

Gospel Canticle

Nunc Dimittis (The Song of Simeon)

Save us, O Lord, while waking,
and guard us while sleeping,
that awake we may watch with Christ
and asleep may rest in peace.

1   Now, Lord, you let your servant go in peace:
     your word has been fulfilled.

2   My own eyes have seen the salvation
     which you have prepared in the sight of every people;

3   A light to reveal you to the nations
     and the glory of your people Israel.

Luke 2.29-32

**Glory to the Father and to the Son
and to the Holy Spirit;
as it was in the beginning is now
and shall be for ever. Amen.**

**Save us, O Lord, while waking,
and guard us while sleeping,
that awake we may watch with Christ
and asleep may rest in peace.**

Prayers

Intercessions and thanksgivings may be offered here.

The Collect

Visit this place, O Lord, we pray,
and drive far from it the snares of the enemy;
may your holy angels dwell with us and guard us in peace,
and may your blessing be always upon us;
through Jesus Christ our Lord.
Amen.

The Lord's Prayer (see p. 38) may be said.

The Conclusion

In peace we will lie down and sleep;
for you alone, Lord, make us dwell in safety.

Abide with us, Lord Jesus,
for the night is at hand and the day is now past.

As the night watch looks for the morning,
so do we look for you, O Christ.

[Come with the dawning of the day
and make yourself known in the breaking of the bread.]

The Lord bless us and watch over us;
the Lord make his face shine upon us and be gracious to us;
the Lord look kindly on us and give us peace.
Amen.

Love what you've read?

Why not consider using *Reflections for Daily Prayer* all year round? We also publish these Bible reflections in an annual format, containing material for the entire church year.

The volume for the **2018/19** church year is now available and features contributions from a host of distinguished writers: Justine Allain Chapman, Kate Bruce, Steven Croft, Paula Gooder, Peter Graystone, Helen-Ann Hartley, David Hoyle, Graham James, Jan McFarlane, Libby Lane, Gordon Mursell, Helen Orchard, John Perumbalath, David Runcorn, Sarah Rowland Jones, Harry Steele, Richard Sudworth, Angela Tilby, Graham Tomlin and Margaret Whipp.

REFLECTIONS FOR DAILY PRAYER
Advent 2018 to the eve of Advent 2018

ISBN 978 1 78140 007 4 • £16.99

Please note: this book reproduces the material for Advent found in the volume you are now holding.

Reflections for Daily Prayer **2019/20** will be available from May 2019 with reflections written by: Rosalind Brown, Vanessa Conant, Gillian Cooper, Steven Croft, Alan Everett, Marcus Green, Malcolm Guite, Christopher Herbert, Tricia Hillas, Michael Ipgrave, John Kiddle, Jan McFarlane, Jessica Martin, Julia Mourant, Martyn Percy, John Pritchard, Brother Samuel SSF, Angela Tilby and Lucy Winkett.

REFLECTIONS FOR DAILY PRAYER
Advent 2019 to the eve of Advent 2020

ISBN 978 1 78140 123 1   **£16.99** • 336 pages

REFLECTIONS FOR DAILY PRAYER
App

Make Bible study and reflection a part of your routine wherever you go with the Reflections for Daily Prayer App for Apple and Android devices.

Download the app for free from the App Store (Apple devices) or Google Play (Android devices) and receive a week's worth of reflections free. Then purchase a monthly, three-monthly or annual subscription to receive up-to-date content.